What Is the Story of the Mummy?

by Sheila Keenan

illustrated by Carlos Basabe

Penguin Workshop

For Kevin, who holds my hand
at the scary parts—SK

For Kara—my partner in everything.
And for Luna and Selene, the two little treasures
we spend our days discovering—CB

PENGUIN WORKSHOP
An Imprint of Penguin Random House LLC, New York

UNIVERSAL.

Visit us online at www.penguinrandomhouse.com.

Library of Congress Control Number: 2021011162

ISBN 9781524788483 (paperback)   10 9 8 7 6 5 4 3 2 1 WRZL
ISBN 9781524788490 (library binding)   10 9 8 7 6 5 4 3 2 1 WRZL

Contents

What Is the Story of the Mummy?

The Ministry of State for Antiquities is the name of the government group responsible for preserving the culture and heritage of Egypt. In October 2019, the ministry sent out a special invitation: Meet us at the Temple of Queen Hatshepsut.

The Egyptian and international press and all the other invited guests arrived at the grand stone temple beneath high cliffs on the west bank of the Nile River near the city of Luxor. Dr. Khaled al-Anany, minister of tourism and antiquities, and Dr. Mostafa Waziri, secretary general of the Supreme Council of Antiquities, had an important announcement to make.

Everyone streamed into a large white tent

set up on the temple grounds. The press jostled forward, cameras raised.

Then eight experts on ancient history wearing white lab coats and plastic gloves slowly, carefully, and dramatically . . . *unsealed a coffin that hadn't been opened in three thousand years!*

The crowd cheered and clapped as the coffin lid, brightly painted with symbols and hieroglyphs, was lifted off. The inner coffin was also decorated in rich colors. Inside lay a perfectly preserved cloth-wrapped mummy.

The mummy was one of thirty uncovered in a nearby burial ground called El-Assasif. The find included the mummified remains of twenty-three men, five women, and two children. The mummy coffins were stacked on top of one another in two alternating levels: eighteen above, twelve underneath.

The El-Assasif mummy collection was the first to be discovered by an all-Egyptian archaeological

team. It was also one of the largest finds in decades and the first in Luxor since the end of the nineteenth century. Even more remarkable: The mummies had escaped tomb raiders and grave robbers for three thousand years! Every one of the coffins was still sealed.

Thirty seemed to be a magic number for the Supreme Council of Antiquities. The week before, another of their teams excavated a different ancient area in Luxor's Valley of the Monkeys.

There they found the remains of thirty workshops and a large kiln for firing ceramics. Archaeologists think this was where the many decorative items, furniture, and pottery that were buried with mummies in royal tombs had been made.

Coverage of the finds at El-Assasif and the Valley of the Monkeys was shown on television stations and spread over social media. Photos and videos were instantly available.

Mummies make good news stories. That's because people in the twenty-first century are still fascinated by mummification, a process that is thousands of years old.

CHAPTER 1
Matters of Life and Death

Most people would agree on two basic facts: All living things die, and dead things decay and rot.

Usually when humans, animals, and other living things die, their bodies decompose, or begin to break down. Microscopic life-forms called bacteria help with this process. They break down the body's cells, muscles, organs, and tissues, like skin. A decomposing body smells and oozes, which attracts hungry insects. Eventually it turns into liquid. This life-and-death cycle provides food for other living things and enriches the soil.

Unless the cycle is broken.

Mummies are bodies that have *not* fully decayed. They can still have hair on their heads or skin on their bones! A body that has gone through the mummification process does not decompose all the way.

Mummies have been found on every continent. Some are accidental, or natural, mummies created by the environment in which the dead body came to rest. In the right very hot, very cold, or very marshy area, a dead body will be preserved and keep some of its solid state.

Pool of ice atop the Alps

The world's oldest frozen mummy is nicknamed Ötzi the Iceman. In 1991, two mountain hikers in the Alps discovered the 5,300-year-old male mummy inside a melting glacier. The body had been preserved by layers of ice and snow. The mummy still had bones, organs, and skin that showed sixty-one tattoo lines! Scientists think these marks may have been from a healing treatment.

Ötzi carried a valuable copper ax and some of the oldest hunting equipment yet found. Two fleas were discovered in his clothes. In 2001, X-rays showed a flint arrowhead still in his left shoulder. Ötzi had been murdered! Someone had

shot him in the back. He fell and
bled to death. Scientists were
even able to determine
Ötzi's blood type:
O positive.

Two other natural
mummies called Gebelein
Man and Gebelein Woman were buried near
each other in shallow graves in the Egyptian
desert some five thousand years ago. Each body
was curled up on its side, with elbows and knees
drawn together.

Gebelein Man

The decaying process requires water. But the Gebelein remains were covered over by dry sand. Hot winds blew across the burial site, and the sun beat down on it. The bodies dehydrated, which means dried up. Their wrinkled skin pulled tight over the bones of their skeletons. Six of these natural mummies were uncovered at the same site in the 1890s.

A moist area doesn't seem like the right place for mummification, but some amazing natural mummies have arisen from boggy graves! A bog is a type of wetland that has peat. Peat looks like spongy dirt. It forms when layers of dead plants build up in the damp bog over a very long time.

Bog mummies are often found by people digging up peat to burn for fuel. That's how Tollund Man was uncovered in 1950 on Denmark's Jutland peninsula. He's wearing an animal-skin cap. His gentle face is so well preserved, you can see stubble on his chin and wrinkles on his forehead. His eyelids are closed as if he just lay down for a quick nap and kept sleeping for 2,400 years!

Tollund Man's full body was squishy but preserved. There were still organs inside. Bogs have a lot of acid, released by the peat and by a type of moss that also grows there. These bog acids soak the skin, hair, nails, and body organs and help prevent decay. The acids help stop bacteria growing. So does the lack of oxygen in a bog. The bog body mummifies rather than decays.

Bog mummies have been found mainly in Northern Europe, where winter and spring are cold, which keeps the bog cool. Most bog mummies show that the person was killed and tossed into the bog. The reasons why are not

always clear. It could be for punishment or sacrifice. Tollund Man was found with a rope around his neck. He had been hanged before he was laid in the bog.

Peat bog

The mummies uncovered in Europe and North America are mainly natural mummies. The world's oldest natural mummy is the Spirit Cave Mummy discovered in 1940 in a cave in northwest Nevada. It is now known to be 10,600 years old. The hot, dry air of the cave helped

mummify the male body, which was wrapped in a rabbit-skin blanket. DNA tests show that he was Native American. In 2018, members of the Fallon Paiute-Shoshone tribe reburied his remains.

Accidental mummies form naturally in the right burial conditions. But there is another kind of mummification process—and it is definitely *not* an accident!

CHAPTER 2
Ready for Eternity

Artificial mummies have been carefully preserved on purpose. They are corpses that were embalmed, or specially treated to stop or slow down decay.

Ancient cultures around the world practiced mummification. People figured out how to use different methods and materials to embalm their dead. Bodies could be hollowed out, the skin stuffed with ash, grass, sand, or cloth, and then all of it covered with resin or plant sap. Corpses could also be dried out in hot sunlight or smoked. They could be freeze-dried in extremely dry, cold weather or "tanned" like leather, using chemicals found in nature.

People then buried or stored these preserved

bodies in special or hidden places to keep the mummies safe and intact. Scientists think mummification is connected to people's religious beliefs. How bodies were preserved and what objects were buried with them reflected ideas about a crossover from life to death to eternal life. Mummies were important and usually sacred to the people who made them—and still are to their descendants.

Entrance to the Spirit Cave

Mummy's the Word

The English word *mummy* is wrapped in word history. It came from several combinations of much older Persian, Arabic, and Latin words. Those words described things that people mistakenly thought were used in embalming, like wax or a tar-like substance called bitumen. The word *mummy*—meaning a preserved dead body— was first used around 1615, and came from the medieval word *mumia*.

The oldest artificial mummies in the world are really old—seven thousand years old!

And they *weren't* found in Egypt.

The Chinchorro people lived along the coast of South America, from southern Peru to northern Chile. This is part of the Atacama Desert plateau, one of the driest places on earth. Around 5000 BC, the Chinchorro started mummifying dead men, women, and children.

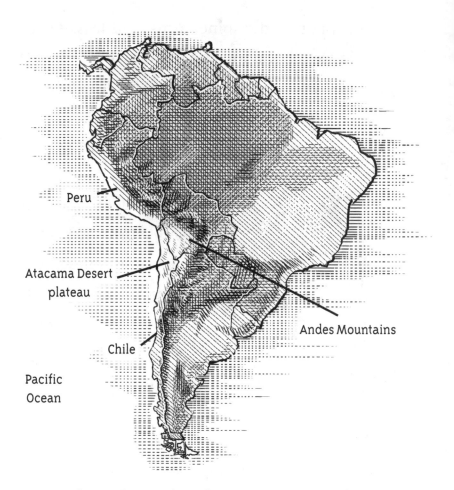

Peru

Atacama Desert plateau

Chile

Pacific Ocean

Andes Mountains

In the earliest Chinchorro mummies, the skin and organs were first removed with stone tools and sharpened pelican beaks. The body was stuffed with plants, feathers, and other material;

sticks supported the spine, arms, and legs. Then the skin went back on. The mummy was painted black and given a wig and a clay mask with eye, nose, and mouth holes. Other mummification methods covered the outside of the preserved body with a red color or with clay. Scientists think the Chinchorro honored their mummies by keeping them upright in homes or villages, before eventually burying them.

Thousands of years later another South American culture, the Inca, also practiced mummification. The Inca were a powerful empire of the fifteenth century. Their emperor lived in the Inca capital, Cuzco, eleven thousand feet up in the Andes Mountains of Peru. The Inca embalmed their emperors and their wives as a form of ancestor worship. They believed these royal mummies still had the power of living rulers. The Inca emperor mummies were kept in temple rooms, often in a seated position. They were richly dressed, wore gold jewelry, and were surrounded by other treasures. They even had servants to fan away flies. The

Inca paraded these mummies for special ceremonies and consulted them about crops and marriages. Family members interpreted their "answers."

In 1995, a well-preserved natural Inca mummy was discovered more than twenty thousand feet up in the Andes. A volcano had erupted nearby.

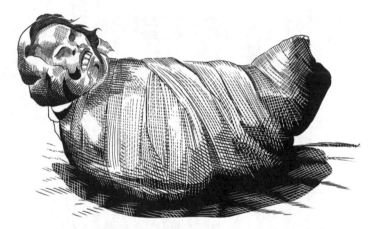

Its hot ash helped uncover "Juanita." The five-hundred-year-old mummified Inca girl wore a red-and-white shawl and a hat made from bird feathers. She had a handkerchief in her pocket; gold, jewelry, and even little clay llamas had been buried with her. The cold, thin air at high altitude froze her solid, inside and out. She was nicknamed "Ice Maiden." Scientists have determined that Juanita, like other child mummies found near her, was a sacrifice to the Inca mountain gods.

Two years earlier, on the other side of the world, the "Siberian Ice Maiden" had been found in a grave in western Siberia near the Russian-Chinese border. She was embalmed and buried there in the fifth century BC. Her body was stuffed with grass, peat, bark, and wool and her eye sockets filled with fur; there were several tattoos of fantastical horned creatures on her arm, shoulder, and thumb. She wore striped wool-and-silk clothes. The mummy had been placed

Burial site of Siberian Ice Maiden mummy

in a very long carved log coffin so that her three-foot-high felt headdress would fit. The coffin was inside a wooden burial chamber, along with the remains of six horses, there to carry the princess to her afterlife. The tree rings on the coffin and burial chamber helped scientists determine when "The Lady," as the mummy is sometimes called, was entombed: nearly 2,500 years ago.

Mummification methods varied from place to place and people to people. But one ancient culture took the practice to a whole other level!

CHAPTER 3
Mummy Masters

If "mummy masters" was a *Jeopardy!* clue, the answer would be: "Who are the ancient Egyptians?"

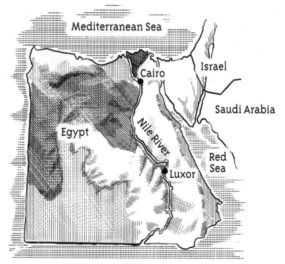

The kingdoms of Egypt grew up along the Nile River from 3100 to 30 BC. During this period of three thousand years, the Egyptians developed mummification from simply covering bodies in desert sand to elaborately embalming and entombing their dead. They believed a person's body had to be preserved so the spirit it contained could continue in the afterlife.

Egyptian priests performed prayers at every stage of mummification, which was a sacred process. Embalming required many steps and took about seventy days. The brain was pulled out through the nose using special bronze rods, hooks, and spoons. It was thrown out as worthless.

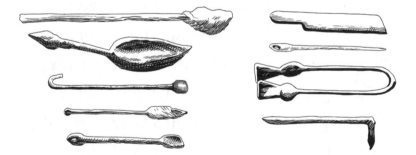

Because they would decay, internal organs were removed and placed in special jars, called canopic jars, or preserved and put back into the body.

The heart was left inside. The Egyptians believed the heart was the essence of a person. The gods weighed a heart against a feather of truth to decide a person's fate in the afterlife.

The dead body was covered with a salt called natron for about forty days. Natron killed any bacteria and dried out the body. The dried corpse was then washed. It was stuffed with cloth and sand to give it shape. The outside was rubbed with resin, oils, and spices. Now the body was ready for wrapping.

Strips of linen fabric were tightly laced over, under, and across the embalmed body. Sometimes the strips formed complicated crisscross patterns. Each finger or toe might be wrapped separately. The body was then covered in a large cloth called a shroud. The layers of shroud and strips were covered with resin. Sacred protective charms called amulets were wrapped into the layers, too. A painted or gold mask of the dead person might be added, and the mummy might be adorned with jewelry like rings, bracelets, or necklaces.

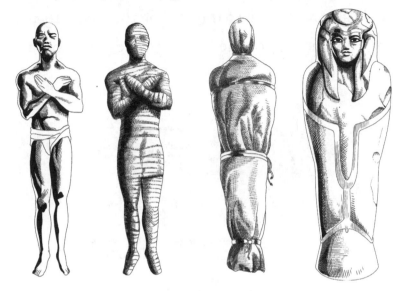

The process of mummification

Egyptian pharaohs (kings), other members of the royal family, high priests, and wealthy people prepared for death for a long time. Craftsmen and artists carved and painted beautiful coffins for their mummies. There could be several coffins nested inside one another, each with a carved face and wig. Some inner mummy coffin covers were covered in gold. The outer coffin was decorated in brightly colored scenes and divine symbols, such as a wedjat eye, the eye of the god Horus, for good health, or the scarab beetle, a symbol of life after death.

The eye of Horus

Some Egyptian mummy coffins were placed in a sarcophagus, which is a huge stone coffin. A sarcophagus could be shaped like a large box or rounded to look like a mummy coffin. It could weigh over nine thousand pounds! Because this stone coffin was so heavy, expensive, and hard to move, a sarcophagus was usually only created for the mummy of a pharaoh or a rich, important Egyptian.

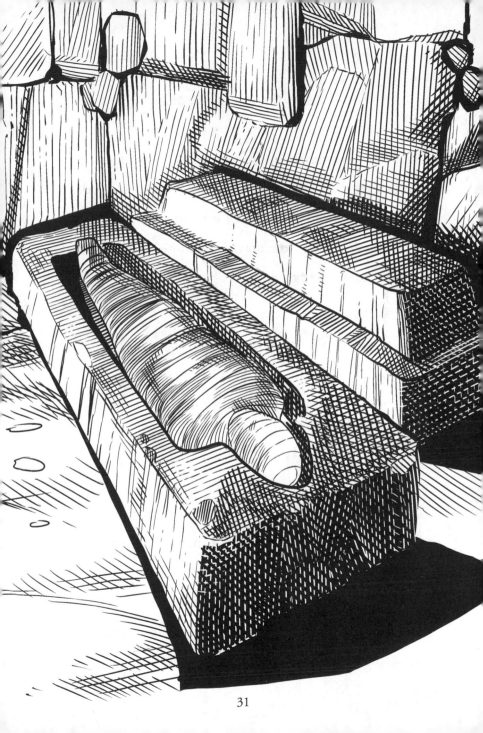

31

Cats, Cubs, and Crocs

In November 2019, an unusual find in a cemetery in Saqqara, Egypt, was revealed: mummies of lion cubs. They were uncovered along with twenty-five decorated wooden boxes filled with mummified cats.

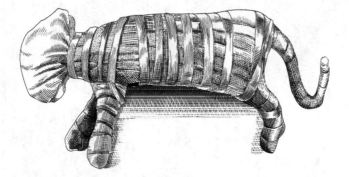

Lions might be rare in Egypt, but animal mummies are not. The ancient Egyptians mummified countless creatures, big and small. Favorite pets were mummified and entombed with their owners. So were ducks and geese, as food for the afterlife. Many animal mummies were used as offerings to the Egyptian gods. Cats were sacred to the goddess Bastet, ibis birds were sacred to the god Thoth. There were sacred baboons, bulls, cows, crocodiles, and falcons.

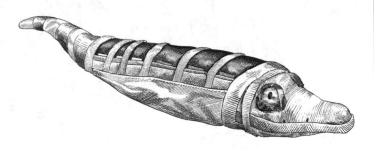

Dogs represented Anubis, the god of the dead: One animal cemetery in Saqqara held about eight *million* dog mummies!

Animal mummification was a big business in ancient Egypt. Some people even sold fake animal mummies!

The canopic jars and the mummy inside its coffin or sarcophagus were placed in a large, fancy tomb. So were gold, jewels, food, furniture, mummified pets, toys and games, and even small wooden figures of servants to do the dead person's work in the afterlife. The hieroglyphs

(picture-writing) all over the coffins and tomb included prayers and spells to protect the dead and safely usher them into everlasting life. A funeral ceremony was performed and the burial chamber sealed for eternity.

Unless, of course, the grave was looted.

People did not always respect the sacred nature of Egyptian tombs. Even in ancient times, they were broken into and their mummies and treasures stolen and sold. Archaeologists and explorers also opened tombs and removed what they found.

When the French general Napoleon Bonaparte invaded Egypt in 1798, he brought a number of scholars with him. The western world "discovered" ancient Egypt through their reports. By the nineteenth century, many Europeans and Americans were fascinated by this ancient culture. But their "Egyptomania" was not always a good thing.

Napoleon Bonaparte

Treasure seekers trekked across Egypt. Tombs were raided and their contents taken for scientific study, for museum collections, or to sell. Rich collectors bought mummies as status symbols. Some of them threw "mummy unwrapping parties" where they did just that. Mummy parts were sold as souvenirs. Some were boiled down to make medicine or ground up to make paint pigment, a color called "Mummy Brown." Animal mummies were used for fuel or shipped to Europe where they were crushed and used as fertilizer.

In 1823, one wealthy donor gave a 2,500-year-old mummy to the city of Boston, which turned it over to their new hospital. The doctor who examined the body cut through the cloth strips that had been wrapped around the mummy's head twenty-five times. He found a blackened face, perfect teeth, and a beetle embedded on the nose. Massachusetts General Hospital raised money by charging a quarter to look at this first complete Egyptian mummy in the United States. (The mummy and its beautiful coffin are still there but now carefully preserved and studied.)

In the early twentieth century, the most famous mummy in the world was found, and "Egyptomania" went really wild.

CHAPTER 4
Striking Mummy Gold

He was supposed to be carrying water, but the young Egyptian boy was digging with a stick. He uncovered a carved stone step. When fully revealed, the staircase led down to the most incredible mummy find of all time: the tomb of King Tutankhamen.

The young boy worked on the excavation team of Howard Carter, a British archaeologist. Carter had been searching for mummy tombs in the Valley of the Kings for years. His financial backer, Lord Carnarvon, was about to stop funding him. When he saw the water boy's find on November 4, 1922, Carter had his crew dig out the staircase, which led to plastered doorways.

Howard Carter

Carter saw the seal of Tutankhamen, the young pharaoh who ruled from 1333 to 1323 BC!

After anxious days waiting for Lord Carnarvon to arrive from England and join in the discovery, the moment finally came. Carter chiseled a hole in the corner of the doorway and peered in. He spied "extraordinary and wonderful objects heaped upon one another" and "everywhere the glint of gold." He saw *history*!

Mummy's Curse: True or False?

"Death shall come on swift wings to him that toucheth the tomb of the pharaoh." Newspapers in the 1920s reported that this warning was carved into King Tut's tomb. Although there was no such inscription, many people still believed in this "mummy's curse."

Stories about the curse spread: A cobra supposedly swallowed Howard Carter's pet canary the day he and his crew unsealed the burial chamber. Not a good sign—the cobra goddess was a protector of the pharaoh.

Lord Carnarvon, who financed the expedition, died a few months after entering the tomb. Cairo's lights went out when he died; back in England, his dog howled and dropped dead. Rumors of the curse were printed and repeated. Over the next few years, twenty-one other people associated with the opening of the tomb were also linked to early deaths or misfortunes, like house fires, mysterious illnesses, poisoning, suicide, and even murder.

Lord Carnarvon

Superstition sells newspapers, but scientists and scholars have found no evidence of a "mummy's curse." Howard Carter himself thought the curse idea was ridiculous. He lived to be sixty-six years old. Yet his obituary in the *New York Times* still mentioned a "Pharaoh's Curse."

The tomb of Tutankhamen is the only intact pharaoh's burial chamber ever found. It has four main rooms, all highly decorated with larger-than-life-size paintings of the pharaoh and various gods. There are hieroglyphs everywhere.

The huge pile of tomb objects included beautiful alabaster stone jars that contained the mummy's organs, gold royal beds in the shape of animals, and a child's chair made of ebony wood, ivory, and gold that Tutankhamen sat in when he became pharaoh at nine years old. Carved model boats were piled up in one corner. There were hundreds of richly painted chests.

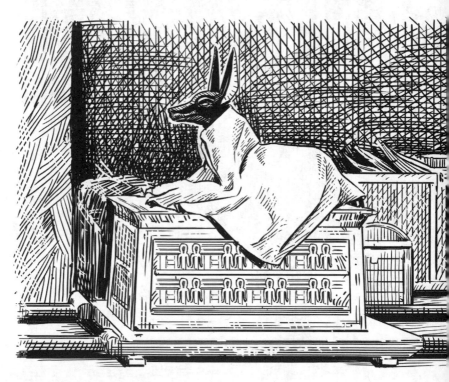

Some held clothes, including the oldest pair of gloves ever found. Another had the oldest trumpet in the world in it. Baskets and other containers were filled with bread, garlic, green onions, and pitted dates. There were jars of meat and 413 statues of human figures so the pharaoh would have servants to prepare all this food in the afterlife.

And there was plenty of gold! Gold statues, gold shrines, gold amulets, gold sandals, gold daggers, even a gold chariot.

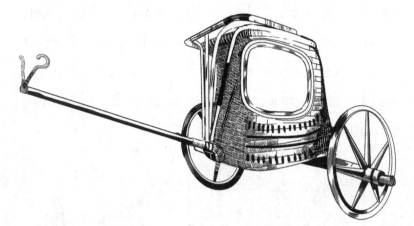

Inside the burial chamber was the most astonishing golden artifact of all: Tutankhamen's nest of three elaborate mummy coffins. The impressively beautiful engraved outermost coffin was made of wood covered with a gold foil. So was the second coffin, but it was even more richly decorated with feather-like patterns of inlaid gold strips and colored glass. The third, innermost coffin was truly fit for a pharaoh: It was made of *solid* gold! The mummy inside was adorned with over a hundred objects to protect it on its journey to immortality—eternal life. Tucked into the mummy linens were gold and jeweled amulets, bracelets, and necklaces. Many were carved with sacred images like the scarab beetle or the eye of Horus, a protective symbol.

The third coffin also held the now world-famous symbol of King Tutankhamen: his death mask. This solid gold face of the pharaoh sat atop the head and shoulders of the mummy. It weighs

twenty-five pounds. The headdress is decorated with gold and semiprecious stones and crowned with a cobra and a vulture head, both symbols of Tutankhamen's power over all of Egypt. The hieroglyphs on the back of the mask are a spell asking the gods for guidance in the afterlife.

The mummy coffins fit tightly together and were sticky from resin. It was difficult and time-consuming to separate them. It took years for Carter and his team to remove and make lists of the five thousand objects they had unearthed in the royal burial chamber. They even had to build a special railway to transport the precious objects from the desert site to the museum in Cairo, Egypt's capital. English photographer Harry Burton took 3,400 pictures of the excavation. Newspapers around the world printed images of the "King Tut" discovery. The famous pharaoh mummy made international headlines—and Hollywood took notice!

CHAPTER 5
Monsters Are Universal

The Universal Film Manufacturing Company was the first "big" studio in Hollywood. It was formed in 1912. One of Universal's founders was Carl Laemmle, a German immigrant. Laemmle owned motion picture theaters and produced movies. He eventually owned all of Universal Studios, as the company came to be called. By 1915, it was the largest film production facility in the world. If you had a quarter, you could tour Universal and watch your favorite film stars or visit the lions or leopards at the studio's zoo.

By the 1930s, Hollywood was booming. More than eighty million people in the United States went to the movies every week! That was almost two-thirds of all Americans. Many moviegoers liked the thrill of a scary movie, and Universal Studios was ready to please them.

Carl Laemmle's son, Carl Jr., was the man behind the monsters. He saw that making horror movies could be profitable. The studio had already been successful with two scary silent films: *The Hunchback of Notre Dame* (1923) and *The Phantom of the Opera* (1925).

The Phantom of the Opera, 1925

When Carl Laemmle Jr. and Universal added sound to their movies, they proved that bringing the dead—or the *un*dead—to life made for big business at the box office.

Dracula was Universal Studios' first horror movie with sound. The 1931 film about a bloodsucking, undead vampire was based on a popular Broadway play. That play had been inspired by the novel *Dracula*, by Bram Stoker.

Dracula, 1931

Bela Lugosi, the star of both the play and the movie, used his deep Hungarian accent to make

Count Dracula sound courtly and chilling. He hypnotized the audience with his scary stare. The Universal movie was a hit. When it opened in New York City, fifty thousand tickets were sold in only forty-eight hours. *Dracula* is now considered a film classic.

Ten months later, *Frankenstein* also premiered in New York City. Universal's next great horror movie followed a similar path from novel to

Frankenstein, 1931

play to film. British writer Mary Shelley created the original story, *Frankenstein; or, the Modern Prometheus* in 1818. In it a scientist brings to life a monster he made from parts of dead bodies. The big flat head, deep hooded eyes, and scarred face of the movie monster became the famous Frankenstein look. Universal's film was wildly successful. And it launched a monster star: Boris Karloff!

Now Universal was ready to transform real history into movie legend. The King Tut discoveries and the popularity of all things Egyptian were about to be wrapped up in . . . *The Mummy*!

CHAPTER 6
It Comes to Life!

"It Comes to Life!" "Brought Back to Live, Love, and Kill!" The movie posters and trailers were meant to send chills down your spine—and make you rush out to see Universal's latest horror thriller.

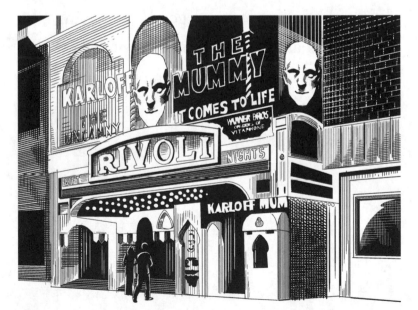

The Mummy opened on December 22, 1932. It was inspired by the excavation of King Tutankhamen's tomb, which the movie's screenwriter had personally witnessed. John L. Balderston was a reporter who had covered the King Tut story for a New York newspaper. He was at the excavation site when Tut's tomb was opened. It was Balderston's idea to set the story of *The Mummy* in Egypt and name the main mummy character Imhotep.

John L. Balderston

A flashback in the movie reveals that a mysterious Egyptian man, Ardath Bey, is actually an ancient Egyptian mummy named Imhotep. In this terrifying scene, Imhotep is mummified and buried *alive* for the crime of stealing a sacred scroll and trying to bring the woman he loves back to life.

Brought back from the dead by archaeologists, Bey is searching for his long-lost love, a princess whom he believes has also been brought back as a young woman in the city of Cairo. The movie is filled with spells, amulets, and plenty

of ancient Egyptian artifacts and images. Key scenes are set in a Cairo museum, including the dramatic ending, where the reincarnated princess begs a statue of an Egyptian goddess to save her from Imhotep.

Imhotep Who?

Imhotep was a real person who lived in Egypt around 2667–2600 BC. He was an important government official and a renowned healer who practiced, studied, and wrote about medicine. He was also a brilliant high priest, an astronomer, an inventor, and an architect.

Imhotep designed the first pyramid in Egypt, which was built in Saqqara. It was the world's first massive structure made of stone. Imhotep's stone step pyramid had a huge impact on ancient architecture.

The Egyptians later made Imhotep a god in honor of his wisdom and talents. There were cults and temples devoted to him and statues that show him seated, studying a papyrus scroll.

The plot of *The Mummy* played into the public's fascination with King Tut and a "mummy's curse." The movie's opening scene is of an excavation site in Egypt. An ancient chest, covered with warnings in hieroglyphs, has just been uncovered. An archaeologist's assistant on the dig does exactly what the warnings caution against: He opens the box.

The young man finds a scroll inside. His lips move as he silently deciphers what it says: It's a spell to bring the dead to life. The camera cuts to

THIS IS
The SCROLL of THOTH.

Herein are set down the
magic words by which
Isis raised Osiris from
the dead.

what's behind him—a frightening mummy stacked upright against the wall. The mummy's eyes, just slits in a gruesomely wrinkled face, slowly open. The camera pans down in a close-up of the mummy's crossed arms. They slowly fall free from their flaking, tattered cloth wraps. The assistant is still reading. He does not see the dried hand wearing a large scarab ring reach for the scroll . . .

There is a sudden scream!

The scroll is slowly pulled off-screen.

Long, dirty strands of linen cloth trail away

through a shadowy doorway.

This now-famous movie scene is all the more frightening because it is eerily quiet, with only the sound of the young man's breathing, until he shrieks at the sight of the mummy. It's a short but powerful scene that only lasts about a minute and a half. But it took nearly eight *hours* for actor Boris Karloff to become "mummified" in his movie makeup.

Jack Pierce, the makeup artist who had once transformed Karloff into another grotesque monster, Frankenstein, was the man behind the mummy. Pierce put Karloff in full-body mummy makeup, even though the brief film scene would only focus on his face, arms, and hands.

The actor was wrapped, mummy-style, in 150 feet of cloth strips. Some of these strips had been boiled until they fell apart. Other bandages were soaked in acid and then burned in an oven for effect. Then he was covered in a thin coat of clay.

When that dried, Pierce started adding the details
to the hands and face, using cotton, glue, and
makeup. By the time Pierce was finished, Boris
Karloff couldn't move his facial muscles or speak.
He really was like a mummy!

For most of the movie, Karloff played Ardath
Bey, wearing a long tunic and a fez, a type of felt
hat with a tassel. For these scenes, Pierce covered

the actor's face in a mixture of cotton and clay and other substances. Karloff's distinctive face grew tight with wrinkles when it dried.

Boris Karloff as Ardath Bey

Karl Freund, the movie's director, had worked in the film industry in Germany in the 1920s and helped develop new camera techniques. He was a master at using odd angles, unusual lighting, and dark shadows to create a feeling of suspense. Freund also was very creative when it came to

close-ups and special effects. He used a small pencil flashlight to make Karloff's eyes appear quite hypnotizing when he stared at his victims.

The 1932 film was a box office success and still has many fans. In 1997, a rare film poster of *The Mummy* sold for $453,000.

CHAPTER 7
Classic Mummy

The Mummy helped prove that monsters can make a lot of money. Carl Laemmle Jr. kept the cameras rolling, and Universal produced four more mummy-themed horror films between 1940 and 1944: *The Mummy's Hand, The Mummy's Tomb, The Mummy's Ghost,* and *The Mummy's Curse.*

These four movies were not sequels to Boris Karloff's smash hit, nor did he play the mummy in any of them. But the plots all shared a basic theme: An ancient Egyptian in love with a princess commits a crime for her sake and gets buried alive. Three thousand years later, his mummy is on the loose, looking for his lost love and killing whoever gets in his way.

The 1940s movies used some of the film

footage from the 1932 movie to recap this storyline. Jack Pierce once again got out his makeup kit and wrinkled and wrapped the ancient Egyptian. In these four movies, Pierce also re-created his hot and uncomfortable head-to-toe mummy costume and makeup.

The moviemakers added more background music in these later films to build the horror and suspense. Some key story details changed. Universal's 1940s mummy movies follow a formula, but each has its own distinct elements.

Jack Pierce applying mummy makeup

The mummy and his beloved even have different names: Kharis and Ananka.

Like the original film, *The Mummy's Hand* (1940) takes place in Cairo, Egypt.

Two American archaeologists buy a broken old jar in the market. The hieroglyphic message on it sends them on a search for a tomb. A fellow scientist tells them that it could be as important as finding Tutankhamen's. Movie audiences already knew that "Tut" meant the big time!

Of course, the archaeologists and their team discover Princess Ananka's tomb, which is guarded by a high priest and the resurrected Kharis. The mummy comes to life, kills the tomb invaders, and carries off a young woman on the team. One of the archaeologists rescues her and bravely defeats the ancient, cursed monster.

The action in *The Mummy's Tomb* (1942) moves to a college town in Massachusetts, where the hero archaeologist and his family are living. Kharis has secretly traveled to the United States from Egypt to destroy everyone who was on

the excavation team. And the mummy is accompanied by another high priest who has taken a job as the local cemetery caretaker.

Showing close-ups of newspaper headlines—*"Witchcraft Revived in New England," "Reign*

of Terror Ends in Flames"—help move the story along. The movie ends in a huge fire in which the mummy goes up in flames. *Or does he?*

This mummy movie stars one of the great Hollywood horror actors, Lon Chaney Jr.—though he doesn't get to do much expressive acting. Without the movie credits, you wouldn't even know it's him underneath all those mummy wrappings!

Lon Chaney Jr. returns in *The Mummy's Ghost* (1944). The mummy Kharis still looks a bit ragged. One of his arms, held tightly across his chest, is useless. He often limps along sideways and sometimes only has one eye open. But he and another high priest are on a mission in Massachusetts. They want to get back the coffin of Ananka and return with it to Egypt. But there's no mummy in the coffin. Ananka has come back to life as a college student's Egyptian American girlfriend.

Eventually, Kharis kidnaps the girlfriend and slogs into the town's swamp, as the young woman he's carrying slowly mummifies. The ancient couple sinks beneath the murky water, together at last.

The Mummy's Curse (1944), the last film in Universal's original mummy series, also stars Lon Chaney Jr. and takes place near the swamp.

Despite the superstition of local workmen, the swamp is going to be drained. Archaeologists show up who want to then excavate Kharis and

Ananka. One of them is secretly an Egyptian high priest. Ananka emerges from the swamp, and the sun turns her into a beautiful woman again. The mummy also rises up out of the mud and goes looking for her. He limps along, dragging his

mummy linens and causing trouble wherever he goes. In the end, the high priest changes Ananka back into a mummy, and Kharis gets buried alive.

After all this mummy drama, Universal turned to comedy with *Abbott and Costello Meet*

the Mummy (1955). The popular radio comedy team Bud Abbott and Lou Costello had already met Frankenstein, the Invisible Man, Dr. Jekyll and Mr. Hyde, and "the Killer, Boris Karloff" in other Universal movies. In this funny horror spoof, Abbott and Costello get mixed up with murder, a mummy, and a sacred medallion with clues to a tomb treasure. When the mummy, now called Klaris, finally awakens, it's only seen in about eight minutes of the film. The movie is mostly silly pranks, misunderstandings, and jokes by Abbott and Costello.

Through its mummy movies, Universal brought to life another great horror character for all time—even though their creepy, cloth-wrapped villain eventually ended up in a comedy film. But after the mid-1950s, the studio let the mummy stay at rest.

CHAPTER 8
Out of the Tomb . . . Again!

Once Universal stopped making mummy movies, Hammer Films, a British movie studio, kept the legend alive. They made four mummy movies, starting with *The Mummy* in 1959. Advertised as "nerve-shattering shock," it starred a famous Hammer acting team, Peter Cushing and Christopher Lee.

The Hammer studio followed up with *The Curse of the Mummy's Tomb* ("Half-bone, half-bandage, and all blood-curdling horror"), *The Mummy's Shroud* ("Beware the beat of the cloth-wrapped feet"), and *Blood from the Mummy's Tomb* ("A severed hand beckons from an open grave"). Hammer's low-budget, bloody horror movies were filmed in "all new Technicolor." Audiences loved them.

After Hammer's last mummy movie in 1971, the undead ancient one pretty much stayed in his tomb for almost thirty years. Then Universal started thinking about bringing him back to life. They ended up with a monster hit: the *Mummy* movie trilogy.

Screenwriter and film director Stephen Sommers had been terrified as a child when he watched Boris Karloff's chilling performance in *The Mummy*. But as an adult working in the movie industry, he knew it was time to transform the living corpse into a new type of character. He had ideas about how to expand the story using exciting special-effects technology. Sommers convinced Universal executives that "no one wants to see a B movie about a monster you can unwrap, outrun, or use as toilet paper." The success of Universal's *Mummy* trilogy proved his point.

In 1999, computer-generated imagery (CGI) was a fairly new technology in feature films. It was used to fantastic effect in *The Mummy* to create howling sandstorms, a plague of locusts, and an army of skeleton warriors. Sommers's film cost $62 million to produce. The budget for the original 1932 mummy movie was only around $196,000.

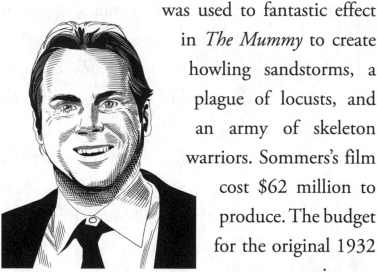

Stephen Sommers

The story features a swashbuckling adventurer (Brendan Fraser) who teams up with a spunky librarian (Rachel Weisz) and her goofy brother against a team of American explorers who are competing to find a legendary tomb filled with treasure. Their greatest prize: a magical solid-gold Egyptian book. The archaeological site they find is cursed because it's the burial tomb of Imhotep.

And, of course: The mummy awakens!
Only this time, he's a horrible-looking creature,
all ragged skin and bones with a crooked jaw
and scarab beetles crawling around in his cheek.

He rebuilds himself by absorbing the flesh and
organs of the living until he is the all-powerful
Imhotep once again. The actor Arnold Vosloo
plays Imhotep as a character out for revenge for
losing his true love and driven by desire to bring
his ancient princess back to life.

Filming *The Mummy* was tough work. Many of the scenes were shot over six weeks in the Sahara desert in Morocco. Sandstorms—*real* ones—often interfered with the filmmaking. The cast was warned: Deserts are home to spiders, snakes, and scorpions, all of which bite—so watch out. But it was all worth it when *The Mummy* opened as a box office success on May 7, 1999. Universal approved plans for a sequel the following morning.

Two years later, the cast was back together in *The Mummy Returns* (2001). Costarring with all of them were hundreds of real scorpions and tarantulas.

This time, the two main characters are married and have an eight-year-old son, who ends up wearing an ancient bracelet of Anubis, the Egyptian god of the dead. The mummy Imhotep is brought back to life so he can steal the bracelet and use it to raise the ancient jackal-headed army

Imhotep in *The Mummy Returns*

of Anubis, the Scorpion King, who's now in the underworld.

The Scorpion King, a half-human, half-scorpion monster, is played by Dwayne Johnson, also known as "The Rock." The movie launched his film career and got him into the *Guinness World Records*. Although he was only on-screen for  fifteen minutes as the Scorpion King, Johnson was paid $5.5 million, a record at the time for a leading-man debut.

At the end of *The Mummy Returns*, Imhotep's beloved princess abandons him, and the mummy falls into a pit of the underworld. So the third film in the trilogy moves on from an Egyptian mummy to an entombed Chinese emperor.

The Mummy: Tomb of the Dragon Emperor (2008) is about power, revenge, and the search for immortality. A secret Chinese general wants to raise the Dragon Emperor from his tomb so that he can find the potion for eternal life. The emperor wants to kill the witch who turned him  and all his soldiers into clay. This idea was inspired by the famous "Terra-Cotta Army," the real rows of statues found in the tomb of Qin Shi Huang, the first emperor of China. The eight thousand life-size clay soldiers, some with horses, are from the third century BC.

China's Terra-Cotta Army

Jet Li, the distinguished Chinese actor and award-winning martial artist, played the Dragon Emperor. But much of his role as a creepy rotting corpse or an armor-clad figure was computer generated.

Nine years later, Universal's mummy was back, and this murderous monster was *female*! In 2017, Universal released *The Mummy*, though it was not a sequel to the studio's trilogy. The movie starred Tom Cruise as an American army sergeant versus an ancient Egyptian princess, Ahmanet, played by Sofia Boutella. Ahmanet is in search of a giant ruby, a legendary dagger, and *revenge*.

Sofia Boutella as Ahmanet

(Because, of course, she was once mummified alive.) Despite exciting special-effects scenes with angry crows attacking and crashing an airplane, zombie armies, and a giant sandstorm whipping through the city of London, the movie was not a huge success.

Still, with new story lines and new technology, Universal showed how an ancient character could come to life on the big screen and attract modern moviegoers.

CHAPTER 9
The Future of the Past

Explorers in mummy movies often have a mysterious map or an ancient book to help them find a legendary tomb. In real life, archaeologists use modern tools like ground-penetrating radar

or electronic surveying equipment to help them locate archaeological sites. But excavating them has to be done carefully and often with simple tools like shovels, trowels, brushes, and wheelbarrows. Sometimes archaeologists get lucky, though. Just like in the movies, sandstorms have been known to occasionally blow away enough gritty earth to reveal a clue to a mummy find.

Mummy researchers use equipment also used in modern medicine. X-ray machines, CT scans, and MRIs show what is inside mummies without damaging their fragile wrappings. With this technology, layers and layers of a mummy's skin, soft tissue, bones, blood vessels, or hair are revealed. These tests, combined with 3D printing technology, allow scientists to build realistic models of what mummies would have looked like when they were alive.

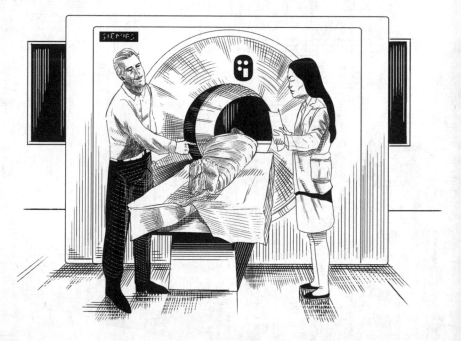

In January 2020, scientists in Leeds, England, even reproduced the vocal chords of a male mummy, an Egyptian priest named Nesyamun. They recorded what would have been the sound of his voice—three thousand years ago! The spooky single sound went viral online.

Studying mummies also helps scientists get a clearer picture of the environment in ancient times. However, it isn't so clear what the twenty-first-century environment will mean for mummies! Climate change is affecting humidity, precipitation, and temperatures in ways that aren't good for mummy preservation. There are predictions that an increase of humidity in places like the very dry Atacama Desert in South America would

Mummy found
in the Atacama Desert

be bad news for mummies still buried there. More moisture could mean mold and bacteria that would speed up decay.

Likewise, if the frozen tundra in Siberia or other arctic areas melts too fast, ice mummies will be exposed. Bodies that were naturally preserved by the cold for centuries would thaw out and decay. As the earth warms, ancient bodies buried under places where buildings now stand could start to rot. Unchecked climate change might make all these ancient remains, whether they are naturally or artificially mummified, age and fall apart.

And that's *not* how a mummy story should end!

Mummies are something from the past that can be pretty useful in the present. Studying mummies and their tombs provides information about the religious, political, or social beliefs of a culture. It can also tell us what tools and techniques they had developed, what natural resources they used, or who they traded goods with.

Mummies aren't just about death. They are also clues to everyday life thousands of years ago.

Analyzing mummified remains can provide details about what people ate, what they wore, their health, their medical practices, or their cultural ancestry. It can suggest when and how humans migrated, or how disease may have spread. It can even link these

ancient mummies to modern groups of people!

Mummies have always been a great source of curiosity. A line spoken in the original 1932 movie *The Mummy* sums up our eagerness to find out the truth about them: "Well, let's see what's inside."

Comrade Mummy

Vladimir Ilich Ulyanov Lenin (1870–1924) was a famous, influential political thinker and Russian revolutionary. In the early twentieth century, he helped overthrow the rule of the Russian emperor (the tsar), established Communism, and organized and led the government of what became the Soviet Union. He is a Russian hero.

He's also a mummy.

After a public viewing in 1924, Lenin's body was embalmed so that it would not decay.

It was eventually put on display in Red Square in Moscow. Nearly one hundred years later, Lenin's body is still there.

Every two years or so, the mausoleum is closed. Technicians give Lenin a chemical bath to help preserve his body. Sometimes he gets a new suit. Then his body goes back into its glass coffin.

The display is maintained at a steady sixty-one degrees, with around 80 percent humidity. Lenin's organs have been removed and his brain studied by scientists. His skin is regularly wiped with bleach to prevent mold, and his eyelashes are fake. But his trimmed mustache and beard are still red.

Bibliography

*Books for young readers

*Anastasio, Dina. *Where Is Hollywood?* New York: Penguin
Workshop, 2019.

*Fullman, Joseph. *DK Eyewitness Books: Ancient Civilizations.*
New York: DK, 2013.

*Hart, George. *DK Eyewitness Books: Ancient Egypt.* New York:
DK, 2008.

*Hoobler, Dorothy, and Thomas Hoobler. *Where Are the Great
Pyramids?* New York: Penguin Workshop, 2015.

*Johnson, Hal. *The Big Book of Monsters: The Creepiest
Creatures from Classic Literature.* New York: Workman,
2019.

Neibaur, James L. *The Monster Movies of Universal Studios.*
Lanham, MD: Rowman & Littlefield, 2017.

Osborne, Jennifer, ed. *Monsters: A Celebration of the Classics from Universal Studios.* New York: Del Rey, 2006.

*Putnam, James. *DK Eyewitness Books: Mummy.* New York: DK, 2009.

*Sloan, Christopher. *Mummies.* Washington, DC: National Geographic Kids, 2010.

The Griffith Institute, University of Oxford. "Tutankhamun: Anatomy of an Excavation." http://www.griffith.ox.ac.uk/discoveringTut/.

Websites

http://gem.gov.eg

www.metmuseum.org

www.nmec.gov.eg

YOUR HEADQUARTERS FOR HISTORY

WHO HQ

| 1967 | 1971 | 1991 | 1993 | 1995 | 1999 | 2001 | 2008 | 2017 | 2019 | 2020 |

Ötzi the Iceman found in the Alps (c. 5,300 years old)

The Mummy Returns (Universal)

Thirty 3,000-year-old mummies found at El-Assasif, Egypt

Blood from the Mummy's Tomb (Hammer)

The Mummy: Tomb of the Dragon Emperor (Universal)

Scientists in Leeds, England, re-create the voice of a 3,000-year-old mummy

"Siberian Ice Maiden" uncovered in a tomb in Siberia (c. 2,500 years old)

The Mummy (Universal)

The Mummy (Universal)

The Mummy (Universal)

The Mummy's Shroud (Hammer)

Mummies of lion cubs uncovered in Saqqara, Egypt (2,600 years old)

rse of the y's Tomb er)

"Juanita" the Inca mummy found in the Andes (c. 5,000 years old)

Photo credits (from left to right): Universal History Archive/Universal Images Group/Getty Images; Harry Burton/Historica Graphica Collection/Heritage Images/Hulton Archive/Getty Images; Universal History Archive/Universal Images Group/ Getty Images; LMPC/Getty Images; JAIME RAZURI/AFP/Getty Images; KHALED DESOUKI/AFP/Getty Images

Timeline of The Mummy

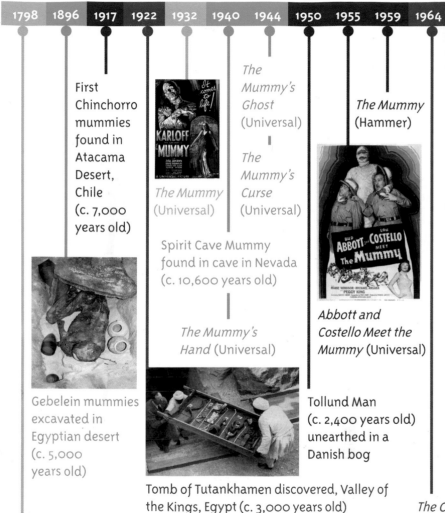

| 1798 | 1896 | 1917 | 1922 | 1932 | 1940 | 1944 | 1950 | 1955 | 1959 | 1964 |

The Mummy's Ghost (Universal)

The Mummy (Hammer)

First Chinchorro mummies found in Atacama Desert, Chile (c. 7,000 years old)

The Mummy (Universal)

The Mummy's Curse (Universal)

Spirit Cave Mummy found in cave in Nevada (c. 10,600 years old)

Abbott and Costello Meet the Mummy (Universal)

The Mummy's Hand (Universal)

Gebelein mummies excavated in Egyptian desert (c. 5,000 years old)

Tollund Man (c. 2,400 years old) unearthed in a Danish bog

Tomb of Tutankhamen discovered, Valley of the Kings, Egypt (c. 3,000 years old)

Napoleon Bonaparte invades Egypt; sets off "Egyptomania" in Western world

The Cu Mumm (Hamr